W9-ACR-612

DATE DUE			

◄ NATIVE AMERICAN PEOPLE ►

THE
POMO

by Suzanne Freedman

Illustrated by Richard Smolinski

ROURKE PUBLICATIONS, INC.

VERO BEACH, FLORIDA 32964

CONTENTS

Library of Congress Cataloging-in-Publication Data

Freedman, Suzanne
    The Pomo / by Suzanne Freedman: illustrated by Richard Smolinski.
        p. cm. — (Native American people)
    Includes index.
    Summary: Discusses the history, practices, and current status of the Pomo of California.
    ISBN 0-86625-606-7
    1. Pomo Indians—History—Juvenile literature. 2. Pomo Indians—Social life and customs—Juvenile literature.
[1. Pomo Indians. 2. Indians of North America—California.]
I. Smolinski, Dick, ill. II Title. III. Series.
E99.P65F744 1997   970'.0449757—dc21   97-9094
                                                    CIP
                                                    AC

Introduction

For many years, archaeologists—and other people who study early Native American cultures—believed that the first humans to live in the Americas arrived in Alaska from Siberia between 11,000 and 12,000 years ago. Stone spear points and other artifacts dating to that time were discovered in many parts of the Americas.

The first Americans probably arrived by way of a vast bridge of land between Siberia and Alaska. The land link emerged from the sea when Ice Age glaciers lowered the level of the world's oceans.

The first migration across the bridge was most likely an accident. It appears that bands of hunters from Asia followed herds of mammoths, giant bison, and other Ice Age game that roamed the 1,000-mile-wide bridge. Over a long time—perhaps thousands of years—some of the hunters arrived in Alaska.

Many scholars now suggest that the first Americans may have arrived in North America as early as 30,000 or even 50,000 years ago. Some of these early Americans may not have crossed the bridge to the New World. They may have arrived by boat, working their way down the west coasts of North America and South America.

In support of this theory, scientists who study language or genetics (the study of the inherited similarities and differences found in living things) believe that there may have been many migrations of people over the bridge to North America. There are about 200 different Native American languages, which vary greatly. In addition to speaking different languages, groups of Native Americans can look as physically different as, for example, Italians and Swedes. These facts lead some scientists to suspect that multiple migrations started in different parts of Asia. If this is true, then Native Americans descend not from one people, but from many.

After they arrived in Alaska, different groups of early Americans fanned out over North America and South America. They inhabited almost every corner of these two continents, from the shores of the Arctic Ocean in the north to Tierra del Fuego, at the southern tip of South America. Over this immense area, there were many different environments, which changed with the passage of time. The lifestyles of early Americans adapted to these environments and changed with them.

In what is now Mexico, some Native Americans built great cities and developed agriculture. Farming spread north. So did the concentration of people in large communities, which was the result of successful farming. In other regions of the Americas, agriculture was not as important. Wild animals and plants were the main sources of food for native hunters and gatherers, like those living in what is now northern and central California. The Pomo were a tribe of seven groups

who lived in the same geographical area. They also spoke similar languages, which all belonged to the language family called "Hokan." These related groups were centered around Clear Lake in what is now northeastern California and also along the Pacific Coast from the present-day Fort Bragg, in the north, to beyond Stewarts Point, in the south.

Origins of the Pomo

Central and Northern California have been inhabited by Native Americans for at least 10,000 years. The ancestors of the Pomo may have been among the region's oldest inhabitants. They were part of a unique Native American culture that flourished in this area for hundreds of years. Anthropologists, or people who study human societies, named it the "California Culture."

Before they came into contact with the white explorers in the 1800s, the Pomo never considered themseves a single tribe. After the arrival of the Europeans, however, the different groups gradually began to think of themselves as the Pomo tribe. "Pomo" was the name of a village located on the Russian River, near the present-day town of Ukiah.

The seven groups, or bands, of Pomo each lived within a small territory that was bordered by one or two creeks. They usually did not venture too far outside their own areas. The Northern or Valley Pomo lived mainly in valleys along the coast, close to the present border of Oregon. They also lived on the shores of Clear Lake to the east. The Central Pomo lived in valley areas among oak groves. The Southern

Pomo inhabited the Russian River Valley near the present-day town of Healdsburg in California. The South-western Pomo also lived in the vicinity of the Russian River, along the Pacific Coast and in the redwood forests. The Eastern and Southeastern Pomo lived in densely populated villages near Clear Lake. The Northeastern Pomo were isolated from the other groups. They lived mostly in mountainous territory east of the Coastal Range.

Daily Life

Pomo villages were small and consisted of six to eight families each. The Valley Pomo built communal dwellings called "brush houses," which were shared by several families. The brush house was either circular or oval and was about 60 feet in diameter. It usually had two doors. The brush house had a frame made of willow branches that arched toward a central roof hole.

6

During the summer months, many Pomo lived in temporary shelters.

The house was covered with leaves and brush. People slept near the walls on beds made from grass mats. The beds were placed either on the ground or on raised platforms. A central space was reserved for cooking.

In summer, the Valley Pomo often moved to the hills because the climate was cooler there. They built temporary lean-tos or brush shelters that were designed to keep out the sun.

The Pomo who lived near the coast built bark *tipis*, which looked like upside-down baskets. The *tipi* had a central pole with a forked top, and long willow trunks were leaned against it. Redwood bark slabs were used to cover the open spaces between the tree trunks, except for a small entryway on one side and a smoke hole at the top.

Every Pomo village had a sweat house. In many groups, it was used as a clubhouse, where the men gathered to socialize and to discuss their affairs. They also slept there sometimes during cold weather. Women were not usually allowed inside the sweat house. It was built like the brush house, but the sweat house was smaller, and it was constructed over a 1-foot-deep pit. Inside the sweat house, steam was made by pouring water over heated stones.

In every Pomo village there was also a dance or ceremonial house, which, like the sweat house, was circular in shape and was built over a shallow hole in the ground. The ceremonial house was much larger than the sweat house. It was about 70 feet in diameter and had two doors leading into the large, central room. Spectators sat around the periphery of the room, on leaves and small branches that were spread on the floor.

Trade between the different Pomo villages took place on their trails, which ran along canyon ridges and riverbanks. Entire villages sometimes crossed the mountains together to trade or feast at Clear Lake or on the beaches. Pomo men were known for their ability to carry heavy packs—up to 200 pounds—on their backs. They used tumplines to help them support the weight. A tumpline was a strap that was slung over the forehead or chest like a sling.

Pomo feasts were joyous, exciting occasions and often lasted for days.

People danced, sang, laughed, and played games at these events. Marriages often were arranged during the festivities. A feast was usually planned well in advance by the chief and the village council. After the date was decided upon, a messenger was sent to a distant village with an invitation. It was a stick marked with the feast date.

The Pomo used seashells, such as the Washington clam found in Bodega Bay, as a form of money. The shells were cut into pieces, and a hole was bored in the center of each one. The pieces were rubbed with stones to make them

The sweat house, in the center of the village, was a gathering place for the men. There, they socialized and relaxed together.

8

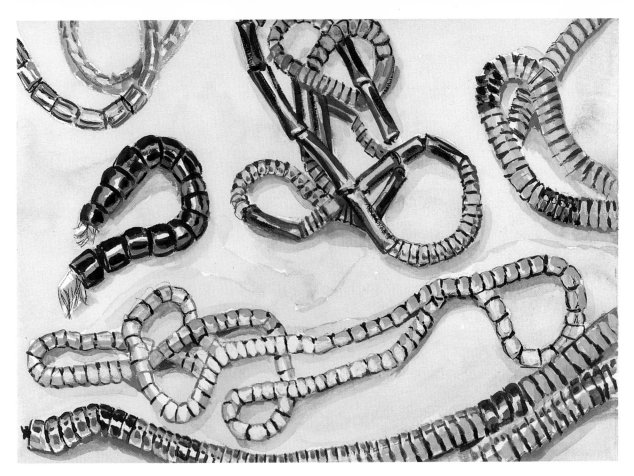

The Pomo carried their bead money on long necklaces, which were worn around the neck.

into round and smooth beads. Then the finished beads were strung into long necklaces.

Cylindrical beads were made from the thickest parts of the shells. These long beads were worth twenty to forty times as much as the round ones. Even more valuable were the cylindrical beads made out of cooked magnetite ore. These brightly colored red, pink, and yellow stone beads were worth 2,000 to 4,000 shell beads, and the Pomo valued them like precious gems. The men mined the magnetite in the hills near Cache Creek, which was east of Clear Lake. The ore was carefully drilled and shaped and then polished against a stone. After years of handling, the beads became very smooth and shiny, and this added to their worth.

Family Life

Pomo families were small and closely knit. The family unit consisted of parents, children, and grandparents. Marriage and children were important to the Pomo because they ensured family continuity. A marriage was usually arranged by the families of two young people. In some groups, however, young men were allowed to choose their own wives.

Once a marriage was successfully arranged, the future groom moved in to the home of his bride-to-be for one month. This gave him a chance to get acquainted with the young woman's family. Among the Eastern and Southeastern Pomo, both families exchanged gifts at this time. In the Northeastern groups, gifts were brought by the young man's parents to the bride's family. The gifts were either valuable beads, beautiful baskets, acorn soup, or rabbit-skin blankets. When the month was over, the couple went to live with the young man's parents, and the marriage ceremony took place. It was celebrated by more gifts and a special feast.

The Pomo considered the birth of a baby to be a special event. In some villages, shelters were built for giving birth. A mother stayed there with her infant for several weeks after it was born. In other groups, a woman gave birth in the home of her parents. Her husband's mother or sister usually came to bathe and help care for the baby.

When a child was a year old, he or she was named—usually after an ancestor. Grandparents played important roles in their grandchildren's lives. While the parents went out to hunt, fish, or gather food, the grandparents stayed home to care for the children.

As they grew, Pomo children were taught the ways of their people. Boys learned tribal songs and played games that imitated the activities of the men, such as hunting or fishing. The boys made "arrows" out of pointed sticks, which they practised throwing like spears. The boys competed with each other to see who could throw his stick the farthest. When they were around twelve years old, boys were given real bows and arrows.

Pomo girls were taught how to gather and prepare food and how to make baskets. They learned by watching their mothers work around the house. The girls "baked" bread out of mud and clay, and pretended to be "little mothers." Girls were sometimes given special baskets for carrying their dolls on their backs.

The Pomo used feathers and shells to enhance the intricate designs of their baskets.

Girls started to watch and learn the basket-making process at an early age. Baskets were valued as gifts and sometimes also used for ceremonial purposes.

Food Gathering and Preparation

The Pomo were hunters and gatherers. Their diet varied according to the season, especially among the Eastern and Southeastern Pomo groups. They ate a variety of plant foods, which were usually gathered by the women and children. The Pomo collected seven different varieties of acorns in the fall. These were a staple of their diet. Acorns that were not stored for later use were ground into powder with a mortar and pestle. The powder was used to make acorn mush, which was eaten all year round. Acorn mush, together with dried fish, was the most common daily meal for all Pomo groups. This was sometimes supplemented with other foods, such as fresh meat, as well as roots, bulbs, berries, and fruits, depending on the season.

In the spring, the women picked buckeye nuts. These were roasted, shelled, and then pulverized. The pulverized nuts were stored in preparation for the winter months. The Pomo also gathered the bulbs of the soap plant, which they usually baked and ate like potatoes. The bulbs were sometimes eaten raw or used to make soup.

The Pomo gathered many different types of berries, such as huckleberry, western raspberry, and wild strawberry. The berries were eaten fresh, or they were crushed and mixed with water. The Pomo sometimes used berries as a flavoring for other foods or to make drinks.

The men hunted for wild game, such as elk, deer, antelope, rabbit, and squirrel. Large amounts of elk and

Pomo women gathered a variety of acorns, nuts, berries, and fruits, depending on the season.

12

deer meat were smoked over an open fire to preserve them for wintertime. The Pomo also ate many species of birds. The bird meat was usually pounded into pieces and cooked in an oven. Various small lizards and grasshoppers were also eaten. Turtle meat, which was cooked over hot ashes, was part of the diet.

Fish was another staple of the Pomo diet. Ocean fish, such as abalone, was dried and cut into long strips. The strips were then cooked over hot coals in an earthen oven. The Pomo ate many varieties of freshwater fish, such as white crappie, green sunfish, striped bass, perch, and king salmon, which could also be dried and cooked in strips. Barnacles were eaten, and were either cooked in hot coals or else dried in the sun and stored.

The Pomo used the sap of the sugar pine tree as a sweetener. Salt was obtained from the natural salt deposits found on the lands of the Northeastern Pomo and from seaweed on the coast. Several varieties of seaweed were gathered for food as well. The seaweed was dried and cooked in an earthen oven and then made into cakes.

Hunting and Fishing

When hunting elk alone, the Pomo used bows and arrows. When groups of men hunted together, they used spears. During a group hunt, the men formed a ring around an elk and then threw their spears at the surrounded animal. Because elk were large animals that were hard to kill, these hunts were dangerous and usually involved much excitement.

Pomo hunters were skilled in the art of tracking deer.

Fishermen used elaborate nets to catch fish on the lake.

The Pomo had several techniques for hunting deer. Like elk, deer were hunted by groups of men with spears. Nooses and nets also were used to catch deer along the trails. Most often, though, these animals were hunted by men who were specially trained to track deer. In order to be able to approach the animal, the hunter wore the head and horns of a deer carcass, and he imitated the behavior of a feeding deer. When the hunter got close enough to the deer, he shot it with his bow and arrows.

The men hunted mountain lions for their meat and skins, which were highly prized by the Pomo. The lions were not easy to approach on foot, but skilled hunters stalked and killed them using bows and arrows.

The Pomo rarely hunted bears because of the danger involved. Bear hunts were usually group affairs like elk hunts, and the men used spears. Some men had enough strength and skill to kill a bear with a bow and arrow.

To catch rabbits, the men placed snares in the bushes along their trails. Sharp sticks, slings, and arrows were used to kill the rabbits. Tree squirrels were hunted with arrows, while ground squirrels were caught by the boys, who chased them and speared them with sticks.

The Pomo were accomplished fishermen, who took advantage of the many bodies of water on their lands. The men used hooks and lines along the beaches to catch a variety of ocean fish, such as abalone, chiton, and octopus.

On Clear Lake, they fished from rafts made out of tule rushes that were

This Pomo man uses a bow and arrow to catch fish from the back of his rush canoe.

bound together. Tule rushes grew in the marshes around the lake. The Pomo who lived near the lake developed elaborate nets and traps for catching entire schools of fish. Spears and harpoons also were used by the lake fishermen. The spears were usually three-pronged, with horn or bone points tied to the shaft. Harpoons had prongs that were connected to a detachable part so that large fish could be caught without breaking the harpoon.

When fishing in streams, the men used spears or nets. They also built weirs, which were fences made out of brush and sticks. The fences were used to drive the fish into a shallow area of water where they could easily be caught by hand.

Political and Social Organization

Among the Pomo the largest political unit was the tribelet, or band. It was made up of a few small villages clustered around one large village, where religious ceremonies and social events usually took place.

Every Pomo village had its own chief. Some groups, such as the Central Pomo, elected a head chief and three subchiefs. Although a chief's position was usually inherited, he had to prove himself a worthy leader. If a chief did not show courage and wisdom, he was forced to step down, and another man took his place. A man did not usually become a chief until he was old and experienced. A forty-year-old man was considered a "boy chief" while he waited to grow older and inherit the role of "man chief."

A Pomo chief had little direct power in his village. If skilled as a diplomat or speaker, however, a chief might become highly influential among his people. He did not give orders and was essentially a peacemaker. His main role was to help resolve quarrels that arose between families and villages. A chief also organized food gathering and trading expeditions.

The Pomo were generally a peaceful people. They did not have permanent war chiefs. Sometimes, however, they fought with neighboring tribes over hunting or fishing rights. Men who were proven leaders or warriors usually led any war actions.

One important battle took place around 1830, near the present-day town of Geyserville, California. The dispute began after a group of Pomo from one village raided the acorn harvest of a neighboring Mishewal village. The acorns had been gathered and left by the Mishewal on their side of a creek. In revenge for the theft, Mishewal raiders attacked the Pomo village, and killed most of the inhabitants there.

Clothing

In the warmer months, the Pomo men did not usually wear clothes. Among the Eastern and Southeastern groups, men wore rabbit-skin breechcloths, which were cloths worn around the hips. In cool or rainy weather, the Pomo men wore mantles, or loose shirts, which were tied at the neck and belted at the waist. The mantles were made mostly out of plant material, either from redwood or willow tree bark, or from tule rushes, depending on where the people lived. Only important and wealthy men wore mantles sewn out of animal skins.

The women wore long skirts that reached their ankles and waist-length mantles that were tied at the neck. Their skirts and mantles were made mostly out of various plant materials, such as rush fibers or shredded tree bark. In cool weather, the women wore animal-skin skirts underneath their plant-fabric skirts.

Pomo men and women usually went barefoot and bare headed. In the lake marshes, they wore moccasins and leggings that were woven from reeds. In areas where the ground was rocky, they wore deerskin boots to protect their feet.

In cold weather, men and women wore animal-skin blankets. These

19

Women and men wore clothing woven out of plant materials, and they wore animal skin blankets for added warmth.

20

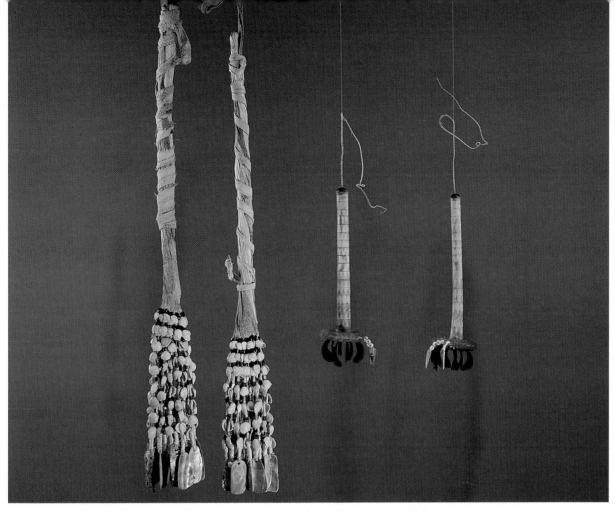

Hair ornaments (left) and earrings (right) made with beads, shells, and feathers, were part of the Pomo ceremonial wear.

were draped across the shoulders and fastened in front with wooden skewers. The Pomo who lived along the coast used the skins of sea otters to make the blankets, while the inland groups made them out of rabbit, puma, wildcat, gopher, and bear skins.

Among the Pomo, both men and women wore ornaments made from a variety of materials. In the Northern groups, the men wore earrings made out of bird bones or pieces of wood that were carved, stained, and decorated at each end with beads. During ceremonial dances, Pomo women wore special fur headdresses that were decorated with glass or shell beads, feathers, or red cloth roses. For ceremonial occasions, the men and women wore belts, neckbands, and waistbands made out of shells, feathers, or colored beads. These ornaments reflected the wealth and position of the person who wore them.

Games

After a good harvest, the Pomo had time for leisure activities, and they played many different games. The most popular men's sport was similar to modern-day field hockey. It was played by two teams on a long field that had a goal at each end. The players used curved sticks to drive a hard wooden ball down the field. The object of the game was to get the ball through the opponent's two goal posts.

A favorite game played by Pomo men was similar to modern-day field hockey.

This was a noisy game that was accompanied by loud yelling and screaming from both spectators and players.

The Pomo enjoyed gambling in many different forms. The most popular was the "grass game." To play, one person hid special sticks under a pile of grass, while others tried to guess where the sticks were hidden. When someone guessed correctly, they were cheered loudly and given money.

The women had their own favorite guessing game, for which they used six sticks. Three of them were marked on one side. After the sticks were thrown, the players guessed which were the marked ones.

Pomo children played a variety of games. The girls made dolls out of wood or stuffed animal skins. The boys spun tops made out of acorns or sharpened sticks. A favorite game for both boys and girls was Jack-stones. To play, a child tossed a stone into the air. He or she then tried to pick up as many objects from the ground as possible before the stone landed. The child who collected the most objects was the winner. Children also played a game with sticks made out of springy wood. One end of the stick was stuck into the ground, and when the other end was pulled back and released, the stick flew through the air. The child whose stick went the farthest won the game.

Another favorite children's game was circle kick ball, which was a great deal of fun. The boys and girls formed a circle and kicked around a ball made out of tightly bound animal skin. Anyone who missed the ball, or who kicked it too far, had to leave the circle. The last child who was left in the circle won the game.

Religious Life

The Pomo believed in a creator God, or Great Spirit, which sometimes was represented by the figure of Coyote. The Great Spirit was also depicted as thunder, in the form of a huge bird with lightning hidden beneath its powerful wings. The Pomo had many beautiful and interesting legends about Coyote, one of which told about the creation of the world. According to this story, there were no human beings on Earth at one time. Only animals existed. One day, Coyote went out alone into the wilderness. It was hot there, and Coyote had no water with which to quench his thirst. He grew weary and sat down to rest. Then he picked up a stick and began digging in the ground for water. After he dug a deep hole, water began spouting from the hole in the ground. The column of water reached such a height that Coyote thought it would keep going forever! At first, the water tasted good to Coyote, but soon it began to taste salty, because it had turned into ocean water. When this happened, Coyote took another stick and used it to draw huge waves in the water. He also drew boundaries in the ocean. In this way, Coyote set the limits of high tide and low tide.

Next, Coyote filled the ocean with creatures that humans would be able to eat when they were created. First, Coyote threw a big log into the ocean, and it became a whale. He then threw in smaller logs, which became seals and porpoises. Coyote formed other sea animals that people could catch from the shore. Then he created the Pomo and other Native American peoples in

the woods. He provided them with plant foods and wildlife so that they would live long and healthy lives.

This legend expressed the Pomo belief that all living things were creations of the Great Spirit and should be treated with great respect. The Pomo thought that animals were their ancestors. For this reason, they taught their children to observe wildlife and to see the wisdom in the animals' behavior.

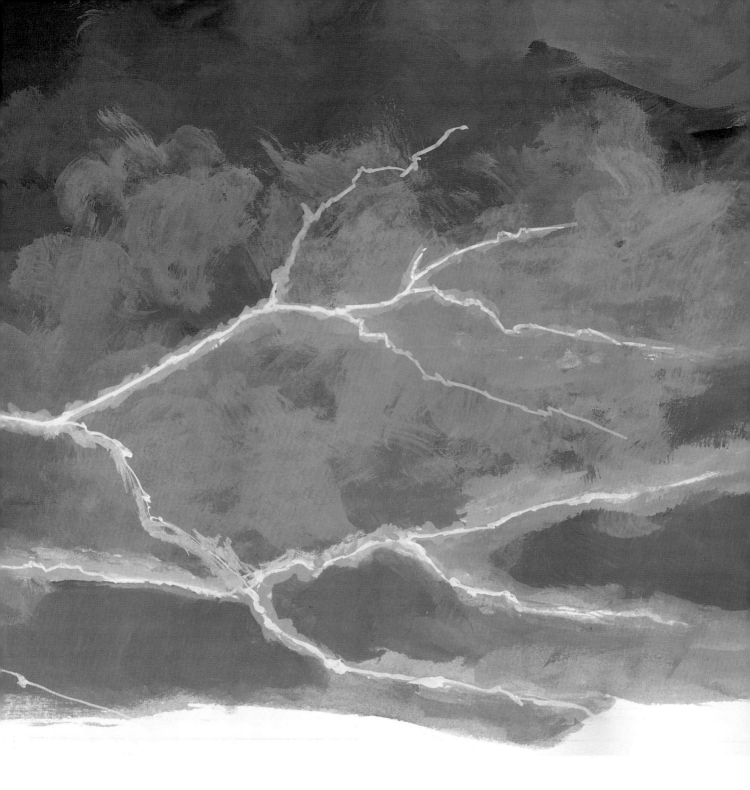

Like many Native American peoples, the Pomo believed in familiar spirits that lived in the rocks and trees. Some of these spirits were ghosts that assumed the forms of people, animals, and monsters. The Pomo thought that most

The Pomo often depicted the Creator Spirit as Thunder, a giant bird with lightning hidden beneath its wings.

25

Big Head dancers are part of a yearly ceremony dedicated to the Creator and other spirits of the earth.

ghosts were evil. To keep away the evil spirits, men, women, and children alike regularly sang prayers.

The Pomo prayed throughout the day. In the morning, when a man or woman went to wash by the river, he or she prayed to the Sun. A man prayed while he smoked his pipe. Some people went up into the mountains to sing and pray. There, they fasted, or went without food, and waited for a vision or dream to come from the Great Spirit.

The Pomo believed that when they died, their ghosts left their bodies after four days. On the fifth day, the body was taken out of the home and cremated, or burned. The personal possessions of the deceased were burned as well, except for certain sacred objects. These were either given to the relatives or were buried. Sometimes the person's home was burned as well. One year after the death, more gifts were brought and burned as an offering to the person who had died.

European Contact

The Pomo first encountered white people in the early nineteenth century, when hunters and traders began arriving in the area. In 1809, Russian and Aleut seal and otter hunters landed at what is now Bodega Bay, in northern California. The Aleut people came from the Aleutian Islands off the coast of Alaska. Two years later, the first Russian settlement was established near Bodega Bay at Fort Ross.

Over the next thirty-five years, the Russians extended their area of settlement and built more trading posts in Pomo territory. The Russians established friendly relations with the local people, who permitted the white settlers to establish a small farming colony on Pomo land. The Russians began trading with the local villages and hired about 100 Pomo men as farm laborers. In addition to supplying them with weapons, the Russians also allied themselves with the Pomo against a possible Spanish attack.

In 1823, the first Roman Catholic mission was established in Pomo territory. It was founded by Father Jose Altimira in the town of Sonoma, California. Many Native Americans, including the members of the Pomo tribe, were converted to Christianity by the Christian missionaries.

In 1834, a Mexican general named Mariano Vallejo organized a group of Native American tribes to help him fight the Pomo. The Pomo chief Saccara and his people fought back, but were defeated. For thirteen years, they were enslaved by Vallejo and his men, who treated the Pomo with great cruelty. Vallejo eventually controlled a large part of northern California. During this difficult period in Pomo history, they were exposed to cholera and smallpox. The Pomo had no immunity to these diseases, which were new to them. Many Pomo died as a result.

The gold rush of 1848 brought many white miners and American pioneers to Pomo country. While some Pomo joined in the search for gold, many others were forced to work for the white miners as slaves.

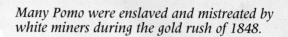

Many Pomo were enslaved and mistreated by white miners during the gold rush of 1848.

The Pomo Today

In the early 1900s, there were few job opportunities for Pomo men and women. They lived on isolated rancherias, or small settlements. The rancherias were kept apart from the nearby white communities. Many of the businesses in these white communities did not allow Native Americans to shop or work there. Instead, many Pomo men and women became laborers in the region's hop fields. (A hop is a plant that is used to make beer.) Others earned money cutting and selling firewood to large organizations, such as the local hospital. Many of the women made baskets, which they sold to collectors. They also worked as laundresses.

During this time, individual Pomo won some important legal battles for their people and for other Native Americans. In 1907, an Eastern Pomo won a court case that gave Native Americans living outside reservations the right to vote. In 1923, one Pomo parent challenged the segregation laws in California, which did not allow Native American children to attend the state's public schools. As a result of this case, and others like it, the Pomo and other Native Americans won the right to send their children to their local public schools.

During the Great Depression in the 1930s, many young Pomo women left their home villages to work as domestics in the California Bay area. Many of the men took jobs as migrant field workers and ranch laborers. In the 1940s, many Pomo men joined the U.S. armed forces and fought in World War II.

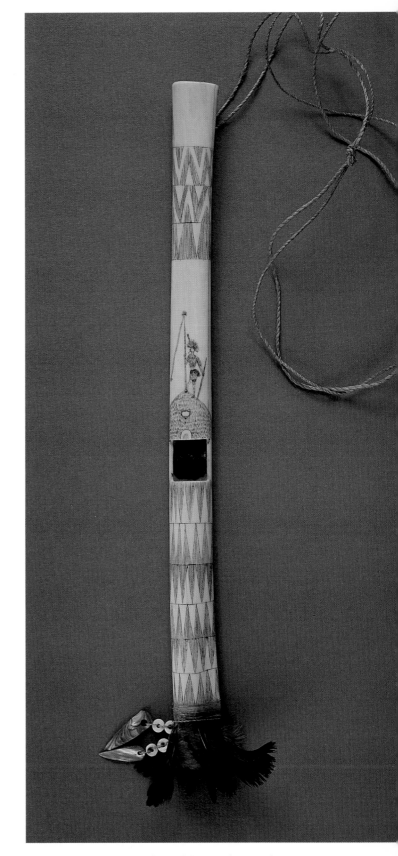

Traditional items, such as this Speakers Tube, are inscribed with finely carved designs and figures.

A bear disguise used in the Be-Sow ceremony is part of the Pomo tradition.

In 1958, the California Termination Bill was passed, which meant that the U.S. government no longer supervised forty-one Native American rancherias in California. Many of the Pomo rancherias were included in this number. They had voted to accept termination, and in return, the U.S. government's Bureau of Indian Affairs (BIA) promised to provide money for improving roads, water supply, and irrigation systems on Pomo lands. By 1970, these promises were not met, and several Pomo rancherias sued the U.S. government to regain their federal status. The Pomo won this case. They also won a case in 1983—*Tillie Harwich* v. *United States*—that resulted in federal recognition being restored to seventeen Pomo rancherias.

While this legal struggle was in progress, members of the Pomo tribe established a farming project and tribal center in Sonoma County known as *Ya-ka-ama*. Today, it is an Indian Education Center and is funded by the U.S. Department of Labor. The center houses a nursery, where plants native to California are grown. It also supports a job training program. The Pomo are part of the Intertribal Sinkyone Wilderness Council, which is a group of Native Americans from Mendocino County. Using modern techniques to restore native plants, the council is working to transform a heavily logged area of public land into a model of traditional tribal land use.

According to 1990 statistics, there are 4,766 Pomo living in the United States. Most Pomo today live on or near a reservation near Clear Lake. Many of their traditions are still a part of their contemporary way of life. The Pomo people continue to learn and speak their native languages and to eat native foods. They participate in traditional Pomo dances, songs, and games. Pomo basket weavers, such as Elsie Allen, Laura Somersal, and Mabel McKay, are known all over the world. Their work is displayed in many museums and private art collections.

Chronology

1811 Russian traders establish settlement at Fort Ross in northern California.

1820s–1830s Mexicans under General Vallejo seize Pomo lands and enslave members of the tribe. Many Pomo die from cholera and smallpox.

1907 Individual Pomo wins court case giving non-reservation Pomo the right to vote.

1923 Individual Pomo from Mendocino County successfully challenges the California school segregation laws.

1934 Indian Reorganization Act passed. Separate authority given for acquisition of land.

1958 California Termination Bill passed, ending federal supervision of forty-one Native American rancherias of California.

1983 *Tillie Hardwich* v. *United States* restores federal recognition to 17 rancherias.

INDEX

Acknowledgments and Photo Credits
Cover and all artwork by Richard Smolinski.
Photographs on pages 10, 21, 29, and 30: ©Peabody Museum - Harvard University,
by Hillel Burger.
Map by Blackbirch Graphics, Inc.

H C STORM SCHOOL